WISLEY HANDBOOK 14

Houseplants

THOMAS ROCHFORD

D1809568

LONDON
The Royal Horticultural Society
Reprinted 1980

Contents

Photographs: Thomas Rochford & Sons Ltd.

Houseplants

The Victorian era will always be remembered as a period when foliage and flowering plants in pots were very popular. The word Houseplant is the modern term for foliage plants which would have included the Victorian palms, ferns and aspidistras. Today, there is a far greater range of houseplants than there was a hundred years ago. Conditions in our homes are so improved with heating and good light that many plants that would have failed in the old days can now live happily in a house. More people are living in flats and with no access to a garden they like to have plants living and growing around them. With so much to choose from, the interest and demand for such plants in the 1970's is greater than ever, and this will continue.

The Rochford Nurseries, now known as The House of Rochford, show proof of the expanding demand for houseplants by the increase of its acreage in the last few years from 23 acres to over 50 acres. Many millions of plants, both foliage and flowering, can be seen in great variety and quantity at the nurseries in Hertfordshire.

The main aim is to help the public to make their plants last a long time and this is done in the form of books, leaflets, care labels and lectures. In *The Rochford Book of Houseplants, The Rochford Book of Flowering Pot Plants* and *Rochford's Houseplants for Everyone* (all published by Faber and Faber) the care of all types of houseplants and flowering pot plants is dealt with very fully.

At Rochford's we have grouped houseplants into three categories: (a) Easy, (b) Intermediate and (c) Delicate. They are easily recognised by the colour of the label. The delicate ones (group c) must have ideal conditions; warm, with a minimum of 65°F. (18·5°C.) and with no great fluctuations in temperatures. Draughts are a great enemy and so is a dry atmosphere. Under or overwatering can be fatal. Intermediate plants (group b) are less susceptible to the above conditions and the easy plants (group a) can stand almost any conditions in a normal house. An easy plant should be able to live in a temperature as low as 40°–45°F. (5–7°C.) for short periods. Even if over or underwatered, these plants have a good chance of survival.

1. Care of houseplants

Apart from the ivies, the majority of houseplants are natives of the tropics and are used to a fairly heavy shade and a moist atmosphere. In their natural conditions diffused light is constant and so light plays an important part in successful culture in the home.

No plant should be left in strong direct sunshine for long periods; if it is, then the leaves will tend to lose their rich colouring and have a pale, faded look which is unattractive. Variegated and highly coloured plants can tolerate far more light than those with green leaves, but it still should not be excessive.

Most people's first question is on watering and, of course, this is the most important operation in the life of a foliage plant. One must remember that a plant growing in a pot is in a different environment from one growing in the open soil of a garden. The roots cannot spread out to the extent that they would if space was available and water does not evaporate at the same rate as it would in the open. The type of pot must also be taken into account. There is evaporation from the side as well as from the surface of clay pots, but with plastic pots, which nowadays are taking over from the clay ones, there is much less evaporation from the sides, so that plants in plastic pots will need watering at less frequent intervals. This is why it is important to have a special soil mix for use in plastic pots, a soil that will rapidly drain all surplus moisture. This is achieved by incorporating a good proportion of fine grit or a fine grade of poly-styrene granules.

Bad watering will not show up at once on the growing plant. Trouble begins in the soil, amongst the roots and gradually works up the plant, through the stems to the leaves.

To say a plant has suddenly gone wrong because the leaves look sick, is incorrect. It has taken time for the roots to die through overwatering and this finally shows up when the leaves begin to look unhealthy.

One is asked so often how to water plants and it is impossible to give a straightforward easy answer, because so much depends on the time of year, the position in the room and the temperature in which the plant grows. It is good to use tepid water or if one can remember, to keep a housecan filled with water in the room so that the temperature of water drawn from the cold tap is raised nearer to that of the room.

To recap on this important function of watering – remember that given reasonable conditions of light and heat, the health of a plant depends on how well it is watered. Remember also that the root action of a plant slows down very much during the winter and at this time watering must be restricted to a minimum. It is difficult to generalize, but one would suggest that during the winter most plants will take only a third, or even less, water of the amount that they will take in late spring and summer. One dare not say keep your plants dry, because one can be taken so literally, and the plant will be given no water whatsoever. In the late spring and summer, when the roots of a plant are very active, they are able to help the plant to adjust to any over or underwatering, but during the winter, the roots are semi-dormant and are quite helpless in wet soil. In this condition, the roots will just rot and die away. Bear in mind that one can always add water, but that it is difficult to get rid of it.

Try to give plants a humid atmosphere and if one can plunge the pot into moist peat it helps enormously. The surface of the pot should always show above the peat as it enables one to watch the condition of the soil for watering. In the summer the active roots like to feel through the pot the moisture given off by the peat and the air around the leaves becomes more humid. In winter by keeping the peat moist, the soil in the pot can be kept drier than if the pot was standing alone. If it is difficult to obtain peat, much the same effect can be achieved with damp newspaper. It is better to give plants water in the morning as rooms begin to warm up then and the plant will absorb the water better.

As a general rule, it can be said that plants with thick, fleshy leaves need less water than thin leaved plants. Plants with thick fleshy roots store up water longer than those with tiny, fibrous roots and consequently need less water.

Plants newly bought should not need feeding, for the nurseryman will have brought them to their prime for sale. Plants which are to be kept in the house, perhaps for several years, do need feeding to produce healthy new growth.

Feeding starts when new growth begins in the spring, and is stopped as growth finishes in late summer. There are various proprietary fertilizers available, specially made up for houseplants, in either liquid or solid form. It is important to follow the maker's instructions on dosage and timing of applications, for a double dose will not make the plant grow twice as fast. These fertilizers contain the required nutrients in an optimum balance for the plants, and an overdose will lead to an excess of salts in the soil which is likely to damage the roots.

It is a waste of time to feed a plant that is growing poorly, in the hope that feeding will revive it. A plant with a poor root system will not be able to absorb the usual amount of nutrients.

Stopping the plant, i.e. taking out the top of new growth, will encourage growth from the side shoots to make a bushier plant. This is not necessary with all foliage plants, for many need no artificial encouragement to branch. Others such as philodendrons and *Cissus* are improved by stopping, which is usually done early in the growing season after growth has started.

Syringing the leaves occasionally will keep them free of dust, and help to produce a humid atmosphere round the plants which they like.

The following lists show some of the most popular plants that come under the three different coloured-label categories: Easy, Intermediate and Delicate. Naturally, the "easy" plants have the largest number of varieties, as most people like to concentrate for a beginning on those that grow easily in the home.

It is not possible to write on all these plants, but some of the most popular of all have been selected from the three categories and have been taken in alphabetical order.

2. Group a - easy plants

Aluminium plant, *Pilea cadierei nana*
Cape plant, *Senecio macroglossus variegatus*
Creeping fig, *Ficus pumila*
Desert privet, *Peperomia magnoliaefolia*
Grape ivy, *Rhoicissus rhomboidea*
Green rays, *Heptapleurum arboricola*
Ivy, Canary Island, *Hedera canariensis*
Kangaroo vine, *Cissus antarctica*
Mexican breadfruit, *Monstera deliciosa* 'Borsigiana'
Mother-in-law's tongue, *Sansevieria trifasciata laurentii*
Norfolk Island pine, *Araucaria excelsa*
Parlour palm, *Neanthe bella*
Rubber tree, *Ficus robusta*
Shrimp plant, *Beloperone guttata*
St. Bernard's lily, *Chlorophytum comosum*
Sweetheart plant, *Philodendron scandens*
Umbrella plant, *Schefflera actinophylla*
Wandering Jew, *Tradescantia*

Aluminium plant   *Pilea cadierei nana*
This plant was introduced from Indochina (Annam) not so long ago, in 1938. The leaves are oblong to oval in shape with silvery patches between the veins. It is a fast grower and makes a lot of roots which need regular feeding if the excellent leaf colour is to be maintained. The plant makes many shoots and these need stopping to keep it nice and bushy. If left unstopped, the plant becomes floppy and leggy. Pileas thrive in a moderately shady position. Cuttings are best taken about mid May.

Cape plant   *Senecio macroglossus variegatus*
This climbing senecio has leaves shaped like an ivy which feels waxy to the touch. The leaves are of a fine green and yellow variegation. It is a

very quick grower and comes from South Africa. A mature old plant will bear quite large yellow daisy-like flowers. The plant requires modest watering and water should be kept off the leaves which could suffer from rot if the water lay on the bottom leaves for long. Constant pinching of the growing points makes for a well-shaped plant. Cuttings can be taken with ease from the half ripe stems (these are one-year-old shoots in which the "bark" is neither soft and green nor yet hard and brown).

Creeping fig *Ficus pumila*
A creeping shrub-like plant, the wiry stems and small heart-shaped leaves are of a good middle green colour. It can be grown as a trailer or climber and will cling hard with aerial roots to a moss stake or wall of a greenhouse. It is suitable for growing in bottle gardens. Never let this plant dry out, but always keep it on the moist side. The growing tips can be removed to keep the plant in a good, bushy state.

Desert privet *Peperomia magnoliaefolia*
The most popular of all the peperomias is *P. magnoliaefolia* in a variegated form of yellow and grey-green. The leaves are very fleshy and store water so the plant likes to be on the dry side and never allowed to be in a wet condition. It is ideal for bottle gardens because it never makes a very large plant. Potting on is only necessary at very rare intervals, but it likes a feed during the summer.

Grape ivy *Rhoicissus rhomboidea*
This is a fairly vigorous plant that climbs by means of tendrils, like a vine. The leaf has three leaflets, the centre one being about 4 inches long (10cm) and 2½ inches across (6cm). The two lateral leaflets are slightly smaller. Young leaves are of a brownish colour, hairy, but soon mature to a dark shining green. Keep it out of strong sunshine and nip the growing points in the spring, so that it will branch out. Cuttings taken from the hard new growth will root easily and sometimes they will root by being placed in water.

Green rays *Heptapleurum arboricola*
This is a new plant of very recent introduction, found by me when touring Japan in the spring of 1972. A tree-like plant, it is all green in colour but the new young leaves open with a brownish tint. The leaves are finger shaped. Each leaf can have up to nine delicate fingers, hence the common name "Green rays." The plant grows very quickly and it can make quite a tall large plant. It is very tolerant about watering, but on the whole, the plant is best kept on the moist side and it likes a semi-shaded position.

Ivy, Canary Island *Hedera canariensis*
All ivies need much the same treatment and the Canary Island ivy is probably the most popular. A good climbing ivy, as a houseplant it needs

Fig. 1. Green rays, *Heptapleurum arboricola*

Fig. 2. Canary Island ivy,
Hedera canariensis

the support of a cane or something similar. It grows at a steady pace, which means it can be kept under good control. The leaves are triangular with grey-green centres and a cream coloured margin. This ivy will tolerate quite dry conditions and never likes excessive watering, which will cause the leaves to turn yellow and fall. Stopping once a year in late spring makes for a more vigorous plant. The Canary Island ivy does best in a well lit situation, but need not have direct sunlight; it is probably best without it.

Kangaroo vine   *Cissus antarctica*
This is another climbing plant supported by means of tendrils and in a pot a stake is required for support. The shining dark green leaves are about 4 inches long by 2 inches across (10cm × 5cm). The leaves are somewhat heart-shaped and have a serrated edge. With this plant too it is beneficial to the shape of the plant to nip out the growing point during the growing season. Fine plants can be grown to a height of 8 feet (2·4m). Repotting need only be undertaken every two years.

Mexican breadfruit plant   *Monstera deliciosa* 'Borsigiana'
This is a member of the Arum family which is by nature a climbing plant.

8

It produces aerial roots at each leaf joint and as these elongate and grow, they should be guided into the soil in the pot. Monsteras have curious perforations in the adult leaves. Watering is quite a delicate operation as the monstera should not be allowed to dry out, but on the other hand excessive damp will cause the leaf tips to yellow and turn brown. A temperature of 65°F. (18·5°C.) is ideal. This is a greedy plant and can be fed in late spring and summer.

Mother-in-law's tongue   *Sansevieria trifasciata laurentii*
Sansevierias can do perfectly well in cool conditions, provided they are kept very much on the dry side during the winter months. If it is over-watered during the winter and the room temperature is low, then the fleshy leaves will tend to rot. Fleshy leaves like those of the sansevieria store up water and that is why it should be kept dryer than other plants. The leaves grow erect, about 18 inches high (30cm) and have a thin green margin with a yellow stripe next to it. The centre of the leaf is grey-green with transverse bands of darker colour. The plant produces fresh leaves borne on the end of a rhizome which is a creeping underground stem. These will appear some distance from the centre of the plant. The rhizome can be severed from the main plant to get a fresh plant, but do not do this too soon. Wait until the new leaf is about 6 inches high (15cm), then burrow down to find the rhizome and cut it three quarters through. This will then encourage the formation of new roots at the base of the new leaf. Once it is well rooted, it is safe to sever the rhizome completely and pot up the new leaf.

Sansevierias like good light and will tolerate almost anything except overwatering. As a guide, water once a month in winter and possibly once a fortnight in the summer. Potting soil should be on the heavy side. Soilless composts have not proved very suitable.

Norfolk Island pine   *Araucaria excelsa*
Probably the best-known *Araucaria* is the outdoor monkey puzzle tree, but our plant is far more elegant. In its wild, natural home it will make a very large tree, but grown from seed, as we do at Turnford, it makes a very attractive small tree for pot culture. The branches radiate horizontally to give a pyramid-shaped plant. The tiered branches are covered with soft light green needle-like leaves. The plant is a slow grower, putting on one tier of branches in a year and so does not need much repotting. Cool conditions are quite satisfactory and watering should be about normal.

Parlour palm   *Neanthe bella*
This is also known as *Chamaedorea elegans* (and correctly as *Collinia*) and is a tiny slow-growing palm with feathery leaves of about eight inches long and each leaf about four inches long. This is a very easy plant and excellent for a bottle garden. It looks very well in mixed arrangements.

9

Fig. 3. Norfolk Island pine,
Araucaria excelsa

It is best to try to keep the plant rather dry during the winter but naturally this should not be overdone. A rather meagre diet seems to suit it best. so only a little feed should be given during the summer. The parlour palm will tolerate a drier atmosphere than many other plants and is never affected by gas or oil fumes. It is a very satisfactory and easy plant to grow in the home.

Rubber tree *Ficus robusta*
The best of all the rubber trees to grow is the one named *robusta*. This is a very sturdy example of a *Ficus* with close jointed leaves. The sturdy stem needs no staking and because the leaves are close-jointed it makes a most handsome plant. A *Ficus* plant will grow in light or shade but great care should be taken during the winter months to keep the plant as much as possible on the dry side. Watering is only necessary during this season at fairly long intervals. From April on one can start watering more frequently as the roots begin to come out of a semi-dormant period into activity.

Fig. 4. Rubber tree,
Ficus robusta

Shrimp plant   *Beloperone guttata*
This plant was first cultivated in 1936 and makes a nice compact bushy
type of shrub. It is a houseplant grown for its shrimp-like flowers, rather
than for its leaves. Flowers are produced almost continuously throughout
the summer and autumn. In early spring it is advisable to prune all the
branches back to keep it compact and prevent its becoming leggy and
ungainly. It will grow in almost any condition in the home but good light
near a window is probably the best position. Keep moist and fed in the
summer.

St. Bernard's lily   *Chlorophytum comosum*
This is one of the easiest and most indestructible of all houseplants and
the proof of this is what one sees in the windows of so many houses. The
variegated leaves of ivory have narrow green margins and they fountain
up like bluebell leaves. Give this plant a well lit situation and restrict
water to a minimum during the winter. During the summer, it will push
up yellow stems plumed with tiny plantlets. It is so easy to increase one's
plants by bending down and pegging these plantlets into another pot of
earth placed near the main plant. They can be held down by a hairpin,
soon rooting into the soil and they can then be severed from the main plant.

11

Fig. 5. Shrimp plant, *Beloperone guttata*   *Fig. 6.* Sweetheart plant,
Philodendron scandens

Well grown plants look most imposing with plumes of plantlets hanging down all round the plant; it is also an excellent plant for a hanging basket. Plants are fairly greedy and make big fleshy roots which can take ample feeding during the summer and ample watering between mid May and mid August.

Sweetheart plant   *Philodendron scandens*
This is a very easy plant among the many philodendrons grown and an excellent climbing plant. Valentine's Day reminds one so vividly of this perfect heart-shaped leaf of about 4 inches long (10cm) by 2½ inches across (6cm). The leaves are of a good shiny dark green. An annual stopping in spring is advised to keep the plant in control and the shoots can be trained down to the surface of the pot and then they will turn naturally and climb up again. A shady position is required for this plant and it will do well in a dark corner. As the roots are fleshy, the compost must be of a quick draining quality. Any waterlogged conditions would cause the roots to rot and kill the plant.

12

Umbrella plant *Schefflera actinophylla*
About twenty years ago it was found that this plant made a very acceptable ornamental houseplant and it has become very popular. The plant is slow growing but given time makes a fine tree of some 12 to 15 feet (3·6-4·5m). The leaves are composed of a number of elliptic leaflets, rather like a horse chestnut leaf. The plant likes intermediate conditions and either a well lit position or partial shade will do, but not deep shade. The compost should be fairly rich and the plant should be fed at regular intervals during its growing season.

Wandering Jew *Tradescantia*
There are many different tradescantias and they are well-known as easy plants. We know of 'Rochfords Quicksilver', 'Tricolor', 'Bicolor', 'Silver' and others. They will grow in almost any type of soil, in any position or temperature; all one has to do is to make sure they are kept frost free. Cuttings are easily taken by inserting four or five tip cuttings in a pot. These are not suitable for bottle gardens, as they grow too vigorously and would swamp any other plants.

3. Group b - intermediate

Blood red croton, *Codiaeum pennick*
Calamondin orange, *Citrus mitis*
Devil's ivy, *Scindapsus aureus*
Elephant's ear, *Philodendron tuxla*
Iron cross begonia, *Begonia masoniana*
Peacock plant, *Calathea mackoyana*
Rabbit's tracks, *Maranta kerchoveana*
Silhouette plant, *Dracaena marginata*
Stags-horn fern, *Platycerium alcicorne*
Weeping fig, *Ficus benjamina*

Blood red croton *Codiaeum pennick*
All crotons are shrubs and belong to the spurge family. There is a vast range of large-leaved and narrow-leaved varieties and a great many colours. Most crotons come in the delicate list, but *pennick* is one that is the easiest of all and so comes in the intermediate list. The leaves are of a deep red, mottled with specks of green. It makes a useful plant, giving colour to a mixed planting. The plant resents draughty situations and rapid changes of temperature. Water requirements are medium and any humidity that can be provided is welcome.

Calamondin orange *Citrus mitis*
The calamondin is the finest ornamental citrus known and makes a perfect miniature tree. Pruning is necessary to make an attractively shaped bush

Fig. 7. Calamondin orange, *Citrus mitis*

and this particular orange responds well to pruning. Flowers and fruit in all stages can often be seen on a plant at the same time. It has none of the thorns so common with orange trees and is almost spineless.

The plant will thrive best in a bright window and it likes a temperature of anything between 55° and 65°F. (12° to 19°C.) during the winter. Watering is most important because if a plant is allowed to get too dry, the foliage will shrivel and no amount of water will alter this unfortunate state. Keep your plant well watered and in the summer it would be wise to plunge it into a bucket of water, removing it only when the air bubbles have ceased to rise. Do not assume that because the surface of the soil is moist the plant does not require water. The pot is usually very full of healthy roots and it is quite easy to be misled by moist soil on the surface when deeper down in the pot the soil and roots may be very dry. Calamondins in pots like to be full of roots and will do very well for two years in the same pot. During the summer, the pot can be plunged in the garden. Let the rim of the pot be level with the garden soil so that the rain can look after it. If there is a drought and a heatwave, then make sure to give it good waterings during this period. Bring the plant in early in September as it cannot stand any frosts, which would prove fatal. Watch for any scale insects which are fond of orange trees; they can be removed by using a matchstick tipped with cotton wool and soaked in methylated spirit, which can be used to rub off the waxy shells of scale.

Devil's ivy *Scindapsus aureus*

This plant can be given the same treatment as *Philodendron scandens* (p. 12). It comes from east Asia and has leaves of variegated yellow and green. Scindapsus have a habit of reverting to an all green leaf and so to maintain the variegation one should pinch out any new shoots that are all green. It thrives in semi-shade, but this must not be too heavy as it is light that holds the variegation in plants. In the winter, it is important to grow the plant on the dry side and to increase watering again in late spring. During the summer and warm weather, syringe the plant with water because the plant seems to take as much water through its leaves as it does from the soil.

Elephant's ear *Philodendron tuxla*

This is an excellent large leaved climbing philodendron. The shining green leaves are shaped like a spearhead and are up to 7 inches long (17cm) and about 4 inches across (10cm) at the widest point. The plant is a slow grower which likes to be kept moist and a moist atmosphere should be provided if possible. During the winter, it is safer to let the soil dry out a little between waterings. Like all philodendrons, it likes to be placed in a shady position.

Fig. 8. Elephant's ear, *Philodendron tuxla*

Fig. 9. Iron cross begonia, *Begonia masoniana*

Iron cross begonia   *Begonia masoniana*
This begonia, like all others, has very fine roots and requires a very light soil mixture. This is a plant that responds very well to soilless composts. It will do very well in equal mixtures of leaf mould, peat and sharp sand with a very small proportion of loam. As much light as possible should be given to obtain the fine colours, but it grows best in a rather shady condition. The leaves are about 5 inches long (12cm) and 3 inches across (7cm) and are green with a touch of grey. The surface of the leaf is puckered, giving a somewhat mossy effect, hence it is not possible to clean it as one does with a smooth leaved plant. Starting from the base of the leaf and continuing half way along the principal veins are narrow purple zones that remind one of the well-known German medal.

When watering it is important to prevent any drops of water settling on the leaves, which may then start rotting.

Peacock plant   *Calathea (Maranta) mackoyana*
This is one of the most exquisite plants for the beauty of its leaf colouring and marking. The leaves are an elongated oval in shape, about 6 inches long (15cm) by 4 inches across (10cm). The top side of the leaf has a medium green edge but the background colour of the leaf is silvery and

16

Fig. 10. Peacock plant,
Calathea mackoyana

diversified by dark green blotches looking somewhat like a peacock's tail. The underside of the leaf is in sharp contrast as the dark green blotches turn to rosy purple and the silvery portion seems to be transparent. Leaves do tend to get brown edges and these can be trimmed with scissors. The plant should always be moist; if too dry the leaves will curl.

Rabbit's tracks *Maranta leuconeura kerchoveana*
Marantas are closely related to the calatheas (see above) and both need the same treatment. They like shade and a warm, moist atmosphere. Marantas naturally grow low down and make a spreading plant. For convenience during transport, some growers train them up stakes and they grow well and look attractive but they are really ground cover plants. Rabbit's tracks have young leaves of emerald green with dark brown-red blotches between the lateral veins. Both these two colours darken as the leaf grows older. This maranta needs to be repotted more often than other house plants because it grows very vigorously. A yearly repotting will be necessary.

Silhouette plant *Dracaena marginata*
This is a real tree-like plant and when it is a good age it will have a bare

17

Fig. 11. Stag's-horn fern, *Platycerium alcicorne*

grey trunk, with a fountain of stiff narrow leaves from the top. The thick leaves are about 15 inches long (37cm), but only an inch across (2·5cm) and are a dark green with a thin red margin. A winter temperature of 50°F. (10°C.) is quite sufficient and during the summer the plant would be quite happy standing out of doors. This is a fine, decorative plant that will tolerate much drier atmospheres than other dracaenas.

Stag's-horn fern   *Platycerium alcicorne*
This plant has been popular for many years and it is surprising that such an exotic looking fern should grow so easily in the home. In nature it grows on the trunks of trees. Two sorts of leaves are produced. At the base it forms large circular leaves that will cling to and girdle the pot. From these pale green leaves come antler-shaped fronds – hence the common name. Since the roots serve more for anchorage than anything else, the composition of the compost is unimportant. They will grow without soil when fastened to a piece of cork bark. These can be hung up and look well in many positions. If you have a hanging bark plant of *Platycerium* in the home then you have to take it once a week to the kitchen sink and let the water run over the bark. The fronds have a greyish bloom,

18

like one finds on a bunch of grapes, so it should not be sprayed or sponged: Repotting is not necessary – it will continue to grow larger and larger on itself. Do not put it in direct sunlight, which would spoil the colour.

Weeping fig   *Ficus benjamina*
This is a fairly quick growing shrub once it has got going and will eventually make a fine large tree. When it is large enough to have a trunk this shows up with a beautiful light grey colouring. The plant has been named the weeping fig because it throws branches without any prompting in the way of stopping and gives a graceful weeping willow effect. The leaves are oblong-oval in shape and end in a sharp point. The leaves are a soft shiny green in colour and the new leaves make an excellent contrast by opening a much paler green. The combination of the two greens is most effective.

The plant thrives in shady conditions and although the leaves are very numerous, one should try to keep them free from dust. During the winter it is natural for the older leaves to turn yellow and finally drop off; so there is no need for alarm when this happens.

Do not allow this *Ficus* to become too dry because it will wilt. It can

Fig. 12. Weeping fig,
  Ficus benjamina

19

be revived by being watered, but there may be a few more yellow leaves to be removed than there should be. The plant makes good roots and is greedy for a rich compost and regular feeding during the summer.

4. Group c - delicate plants

Angels wings, *Caladium*
Dumb cane, *Dieffenbachia* 'Exotica'
Fan plant, *Begonia rex*
Lollipop plant, *Pachystachys lutea*
Rainbow plant, *Dracaena marginata tricolor*
Red herringbone, *Maranta tricolor*
Saffron spike, *Aphelandra* 'Brockfeld'
Spider plant, *Aralia elegantissima*
Variegated trailing fig, *Ficus radicans variegata*

Angels wings *Caladium*
The varieties of this plant are legion and include those with many different leaf colours. The *Caladium* originated from South America, mostly from Brazil and British Guiana. It cannot be claimed as a true houseplant because the leaves die down naturally every winter and reappear again in the spring. But it makes a most ornamental plant in a pot and if bought in April, one that can be enjoyed for a long time. The leaves spring from an underground tuber and will rise to a height of 8 to 12 inches (20-30cm). Most caladiums have leaves about 9 inches long (22cm) and are shaped like an arrow head. Easily the most popular of all is *Caladium candidum* which has white leaves veined with green. To hold the colouring it should be given as light a position as possible and it requires plenty of water especially when the new leaves are emerging. As the leaves fade with old age water should be restricted and the pots stored in a temperature of about 60°F. (16°C.). During the winter dormant stage they should neither be allowed to become dust dry nor too wet. In either of these conditions the tubers will tend to rot. In March they can be started into growth at a temperature of 70°F. (21°C.). When there is a good show of leaves and good root action they can be brought into a cooler position.

Dumb cane *Dieffenbachia* 'Exotica'
This genus was named after a Herr Dieffenbach in 1830, when he was the gardener at Schönbrunn Palace in Vienna. They are known as the dumb canes because biting any part of them is poisonous and will cause loss of speech for several days. These plants are so beautiful they have become very popular and *Dieffenbachia* 'Exotica' is the best variety of all. They

Fig. 13. Dumb cane,
Dieffenbachia
'Exotica'

come from central America and the West Indies and therefore like warm, moist conditions. The night temperature should not fall below 50°F. (10°C.), but they do well at 60°F. or over (16°C+). When cuttings are propagated they need a high temperature of 80°F. (27°C.). Dieffenbachias grow well in a mixture of equal parts of loam, peat and leaf mould, but they will also respond to a soilless compost.

Fan plant *Begonia rex*

The Latin for king is *Rex*. This plant is rightly called *Begonia rex* because it is the king of all begonias. All rex types are fibrous rooted and the leaves all face one way in fan shape. They cannot stand gas fumes and should be kept well away from a gas fire. They like a moist buoyant atmosphere and will do well if the pots are plunged in peat that is kept moist. When potting they need a very open mixture and should be potted very lightly. Do not press the soil down hard in the pot. A good mixture for potting is two parts loam, two parts peat, one part sand and one part leaf mould.

A shady position is best for the plant and the soil should always be kept just moist. Any plant with fibrous roots needs careful watering because the roots do not take up much water. Never try to sponge a rex leaf – they are too delicate to stand this treatment.

21

Fig. 14. Fan plant,
Begonia rex

Lollipop plant   *Pachystachys lutea*
This is a very new introduction and the bract and flowers look somewhat
like an *Aphelandra*. It makes a compact, self-branching plant with leaves
of a good green colour. The bracts are a vivid bright yellow. When these
are finished they can be cut back to a good pair of leaves and new shoots
will soon appear. These in time should produce the bracts and flowers.
The upright spikes resemble a lollipop, hence the common name given
to this delightful plant. It is one of the easiest plants in the delicate group
and will do well in any position in the home, but likes a temperature of
60°F. (16°C.) or over.

Rainbow plant   *Dracaena marginata tricolor*
Just a short note on this spectacular plant, which was introduced to the
Rochford nurseries when found by me on a visit to Japan in 1972, and
shown for the first time at Chelsea in 1973. The main colours of the leaves
are green, red, pink and cream. They are very graceful and fountain out
from a main stem. Although we have thought it best to put it in the
delicate category, we feel it will do very well in the home in almost any
conditions. The only advice given is to give it a good light position so
that its colour will not fade. It is an easy plant to water, but is best kept
on the moist side.

22

Fig. 15. Rainbow
plant, *Dracaena
marginata tricolor*

Red herringbone   *Maranta tricolor*
This is an attractive low-growing plant with oval leaves about 5 inches
long (12cm) by 3 inches wide (7cm). The leaves are of a fine deep green
with the principal veins coloured reddish pink. As one knows only too
well, marantas have a habit of getting brown tips to the leaves. This be-
haves better than most in this respect and the yellowing of the leaf tips is
less troublesome. All marantas like to be grown in semi-shade. They
should be kept moist at all times and given a temperature of about 60°F.
(15·5°C.).

Saffron spike   *Aphelandra* 'Brockfeld'
This is the best example of a flowering houseplant because when the
flowers have finished, one still has a plant with leaves worth looking at.
The plant has an upright stem from which the large leaves, of very dark
green with the mid-rib and principal lateral veins picked out in wide
bands of ivory, spring from each joint in pairs. It takes a plant about ten
months to produce a head of yellow flowers, which emerge over a long

23

Fig. 16. Saffron spike, *Aphelandra* 'Brockfield'

period of two to three weeks from the yellow bracts. The bracts are curiously shaped in a four-sided pyramid, which eventually turn green. These should then be removed and side shoots will develop in the leaf axils and can be used as cuttings or allowed to grow and eventually flower. When the plant is growing vigorously it will need constant watering. Never let this plant dry out completely at any time or season. A winter temperature of 50°F. (10°C.) is sufficient. Mite and scale are usually the most serious pests, but nicotine or a white oil solution will control both of these. *Aphelandra* needs to be repotted in fresh soil every spring. Do not feed until a tiny yellow bud can be seen. If overfed in the early stages this can result in large leaves and no flowers at all.

Spider plant *Aralia elegantissima*
Some people will argue that this plant should be called *Dizygotheca*, but it is well-known as *Aralia*. The thin, spidery leaves are most elegant and are divided into seven to ten sections. The petiole is like a thread and is mottled with white. As the plant ages the leaves change character and become much wider. The leaves of a young spider plant are a browny red, metallic colour, but later as they mature they turn so dark they are

24

nearly black. Red spider and scale need to be looked for as the most likely pests to attack the plant. This plant comes from the New Hebrides and needs the best conditions one can give and a moist atmosphere. It is not an easy plant to grow in the house.

Variegated trailing fig   *Ficus radicans variegata*
Like *Ficus pumila*, this is another small-leaved creeping fig. The leaves are larger than those of *F. pumila* and the edge is slightly waved. This is a very attractive plant but difficult to keep in good condition during the winter. It comes from the East Indies and enjoys a warm and moist atmosphere that is draught free. Side shoots produce themselves naturally but stopping the tips will encourage them still more. The thin branches can be made to trail or climb and are thickly covered with beautifully variegated leaves of cream and green.

5. Flowering pot plants

Flowering pot plants should be regarded as expendable. One cannot expect them to last as long as houseplants, but they have a very much longer life than cut flowers. It is for the brilliance of the flowers that they produce that the comparative brevity of their display is accepted. Once the flowers have faded the tendency is to throw the plant away. If they are annuals, then this is the only thing to do, but some flowering plants, other than annuals, can be preserved and looked after from year to year. Much can be done on windowsills but it is much easier and more rewarding to have the assistance of a small heated greenhouse. Temperature and light are important factors in growing good flowering plants. Atmosphere is also important in many ways. If the atmosphere is very dry, the plant will not develop the flowers as well as when there is some moisture around the plant. Although the room temperature may be correct, a plant will suffer and grow badly if it is standing in a draught for any length of time. When plants grow slowly or have come into full flower they will not need so much water as when in active growth and coming up to perfection.

It is most important with flowering plants to water correctly. Under or overwatering can soon spoil the quality of the flowers. When one decides to water, do it properly. If the plant has been correctly potted, there will be a space of about a quarter of an inch between the top surface of the soil and the rim of the pot. Pour water slowly on the soil surface until it is level with the rim. This should slowly soak in and water all the soil in the pot. If one only gives a little water, it will not penetrate further than the top portion of the soil, which means the lower portion will always be too dry. The roots at the lower levels will become starved because the plant is unable to obtain all the nourishment it requires, and this results in poor quality flowers. Leaves can stand more hardship than flowers, and so there is less margin of error with foliage plants than with flowering pot plants.

Most plants are now sold in plastic pots for economic reasons and in many cases the soil mix has a large proportion of peat. If it is dry, a plant in a peat mixture will feel very light when lifted. One must learn by experience to have a standard of comparison between the weight of a well-watered plant and that of a dry one. When a peat mixture gets too dry it will shrink from the sides of the pot and when water is given it will run straight down the sides of the pot and flow out of the drainage holes at the base of the pot almost immediately. No quantity of water is therefore able to penetrate the dry mixture. The best procedure in this case is to stand the pot in a bucket of water. Make sure the surface of the pot is below the level of the water in the bucket. Wait for all the bubbles to stop rising and this will mean that the whole potful of soil is now in good condition for water.

The azalea is one of the best examples of what can happen in such a case because the potting mixture normally used is almost pure peat. To make it easier to know how to deal with watering a flowering plant, do not water when the soil is already damp, when the temperature is very low, or where the plant shows little signs of growth or development in its roots, leaves or flowers.

Water moderately when the plant restarts into growth, after flowering is over, after repotting, and when the temperature is low (even though the plant is in full growth).

Water frequently when the plant is in full growth, when the plant is coming up to full bud and flower, and when temperatures are high. Bear in mind that even more frequent watering will be required when a plant is pot bound, meaning full of roots, and when the plant is in a soil mixture based mainly on peat.

If one is successful in keeping plants, the time will come when they will need to be potted on into larger pots. The usual sequence is to pot from a 3½ inch (9cm) into a 5½ inch (14cm) pot and on again, in due course, into a 7 inch (18cm) pot. Soil mixtures are best purchased already mixed by reputable firms. The John Innes composts are first-class and can be obtained quite easily. When a flowering pot plant has been bought in prime condition, the roots are most likely to have taken over most of the soil in the pot. With flowering plants, the best time to pot these on is when they have finished flowering. The only exception to this is a plant that finishes flowering in midwinter, which should be held for potting until the early spring.

The best, and really the only time to repot a plant, is in the early spring when the plant is making new and vigorous roots. Through the late autumn and winter the roots have been semi-dormant but become really

26

active again in the spring. For flowering pot plants, the John Innes compost No. 2 is recommended for repotting.

Feeding should be considered only when the soil is full of healthy roots and this again should not be undertaken in the winter; wait for the spring and summer months. Many people kill their plants by giving feed when the plant looks sick. Feeding is only for the healthy plants, and no feed can save roots that are sick and dying, it will only end the life of the plant more quickly. All one can do to try and save the sick plant is to restrict the watering to a minimum.

As a general rule, one should not feed flowering pot plants when they are in flower. Most plants are purchased in flower and they will have been given all necessary feed to see the plant through by the nurseryman.

Azaleas

The azaleas that one sees at Christmas made their appearance round about the 1850's. The art of growing these plants for forcing has mostly been exclusive to the Belgians. Plants are sent from Belgium all over the world to nurserymen who force and grow them to final perfection. Other countries now undertake the culture of the young azaleas, but traditionally the Belgians were responsible for the introduction of this beautiful plant. A great flow of varieties began in earnest in the 1860's when three famous Belgian nurseries were all devoted to working on azaleas. Most of their success came from bud sports rather than hybridization. The early forcing varieties for Christmas are found in the Petrick group. 'Madame Petrick', one of the most popular, is a bright pink. 'Perle de Noisy' is a paler pink, flushed white. 'Madame August van Damme' is a good middle pink. 'Petrick Alba' makes a very fine white. The fairly recent 'Ambrosiana' has come on the market and is a most outstanding azalea. It is very free flowering, with large bright red double flowers. The leaves are of a good dark green and they hold on the plant longer than any other variety. When plants are allowed to get too dry and have to be soaked in a bucket of water, one common result is a lot of leaf drop. 'Ambrosiana' comes out best of all for holding its leaves.

The salmon colours are excellent in the Shäme varieties: 'Princess Beatrix' and 'Paul Shäme' are the best. Another beautiful one is 'Eric Shäme', which is salmon pink, flushed white.

Azaleas are graded and priced by the diameter measurement across the head of flowers. The 11 inch is the most popular size, but 8-inch and 18-inch are also in demand. After January many other varieties that cannot be forced early are available in a multitude of colours. They are mostly from the Vervaenianas introduced by Mr. Joseph Vervaene in 1886. All these lovely range of colours, all increased from bud sports, cannot be forced for Christmas but can be made to flower about late February.

Fig. 17. Azalea

Another outstanding late azalea is 'Ambrosius', not to be confused with 'Ambrosiana'. This is similar in all ways to 'Ambrosiana', but it is a really late variety and serves a very useful purpose to extend the season of this bright red, double flowered azalea. Under electric light the colour looks truly magnificent. One looks forward to the sports which are bound to come, in time, in other colours.

The plants are lifted in potballs of medium peat and pine needles and so dry out very quickly. These are given a good soaking for twenty-four hours and then potted and pressed down hard into the correct size pot. These are set out in the greenhouse and kept at a night temperature of 50°F. (10°C.) for about one month. They need this cool period to recover from being lifted and potted and the watering must be absolutely correct in this critical period. If all is well after four weeks one should find a mass of white root tips round the side of the soil ball when knocked out for inspection. The plants are now ready for forcing and the temperature is raised steadily at weekly intervals. A night temperature of 72°F. (22°C.) is about the maximum to be given; anything higher will tend to make the flowers come on the small side. Azaleas should never be fed with any standard fertilizer. Spraying over the top of the plants helps to produce even flowering, but must stop when the flower begins to show because the water will mark them and tend to set up rot.

When buying a plant it is tempting to take one in full flower, but it is better to choose one in good bud, which will last longer. The buds are best when showing good colour and there is no fear of not being able to bring the plant to perfection.

Watering is very important and, because the azalea is growing in almost pure peat, it will need a constant watch. The best guide of all to watering is to look at the trunk stem of the azalea which rises from the middle of the pot. If watering is correct and the plant can be said to be in perfect condition, then one will observe a dark water line about half an inch up the stem from the base. This waterline is very distinct and rings the stem. Above this sharp, almost black line, it will be quite dry and pale in colour. If the plant is overwatered the dark line will creep up and even get into the branches. In this case one must dry the plant out, but in doing so the plant is bound to drop some leaves and even flowers. If the stem is dry right down to the soil level, then normal watering may not put this right and it will be necessary to plunge the plant in a bucket of water and leave it there until all air bubbles stop rising. If rain water is available use this but it should be brought to a temperature of 60°F. (15·5°C.) beforehand.

Azaleas are tolerant of almost any position in a room; they are not affected by gas fumes but it is best to avoid putting one very near a hot coal fire. When the plant has finished flowering any dead flowers should be removed. The plant should have just enough water to keep it alive and in the early summer it can be put outside in the garden in a shady place. Plunge the pot in the soil and leave the rim showing in order to be able to control the watering. Quite a lot of new growth will be made by the late summer when it should be brought back in the house. It must not be left out in any frost which will kill it.

Azaleas do not like any feeding. They can be potted on into a larger pot when flowering has finished, but if they have been bought for Christmas and have finished flowering during mid-winter wait until the spring. Use a mixture of chopped up pine needles (1 part) and peat (2 parts).

Chrysanthemums

We are now so used to having chrysanthemums in pots all the year round that we have almost forgotten that they were a sign of autumn and winter and were once only grown at that time of year.

One wondered if they would be acceptable all the year round but this has been proved in this country and especially in the United States. The reason why they are so popular all through the year in the States is because they stand up so well to the hot dry conditions of the American home. In this country we know how well they last and it ensures popularity with the public when a flowering pot plant falls into this category.

A chrysanthemum should be placed in a well lit position which is reasonably cool. In these conditions the flower will last for a long period. The roots are very active and the plant is therefore difficult to overwater. When growing in a high summer temperature they can take water every day, but in cold winter weather they take far less; even so they will take more water than most other plants. Few people would want to know how to grow their own chrysanthemums year round, but for those who are interested to know how it is done the following procedure is necessary. After the cuttings have rooted, and this takes about two weeks, flowering can be obtained in as short a time as nine weeks. Place five rooted cuttings round the edge of a five-inch pot and water in. Compost should be John Innes No. 2. Keep the pots in a greenhouse at a constant temperature of 60°F. (15·5°C.).

The plants for the first part of their growth are given 14 hours daylight each day. If necessary the daylight must be artificially prolonged by the use of 60 watt bulbs suspended every 6 feet (1·8m), 3 feet (90cm) above the plants. These are switched on in the morning or the evening to extend the length of day to 14 hours. This is the so-called "Long-day treatment". After plants have been potted for a week the plants should be regularly fed at each watering. This liquid feed should contain 12 per cent nitrogen and 4 per cent potash. The phosphates necessary to the plant are already present in the correct proportions in the J.I. base fertilizer. Feeding should continue until the buds show colour.

Two weeks after potting the growing plant is pinched out and this encourages the side shoots to break. The use of growth retarding chemicals is usually necessary in order to make a good, short, bushy plant. When the long-day treatment is finished, the short-day treatment should begin. This means reducing the hours of daylight to ten hours, and this is effected by using black polythene which blacks out the greenhouse. It must be a total blackout and no daylight must be allowed to get through. The normal hours of blackout are from 17.30 to 07.30.

When a cluster of buds can be handled, they should be disbudded and reduced to one bud per cluster. Each cutting should make four breaks and if this happens one can expect twenty heads of flowers to a pot.

When the buds show colour, they should be exposed to whatever the natural daylight conditions are at that particular season.

Try not to buy plants in a very backward flower condition, because then it is difficult to get them to mature to full size. In the late spring and summer buy a plant with flowers half out, but in winter the flowers must be at least three parts out. With the poor light in winter and coming from good greenhouse conditions into the home, the flowers will never mature if only half out. The petals will go brown and rot will set in. Well developed flowers are the only ones to have during winter for satisfaction.

Because chrysanthemums in pots have had special culture to control height and flowering, it is not satisfactory to try to pot them on for another year. The best thing to do is to plant them out in the garden where they will revert back to growing their normal height which, without treatment, would be too tall for pot culture.

Cyclamen

Cyclamen became important plants about 1900. Messrs Suttons had introduced an excellent strain of good mixed colours. In France and Germany great strides were also being made and in 1904 Meckel's Silberblatt (silver leaf) strain was introduced in Germany. The French and Germans paid more attention to obtaining ornamental markings on the leaves and the modern Silver Leaf as we know it today is a fine example of magnificent leaf markings.

Cyclamen is a popular Christmas plant but can be grown almost all the year round. Plants like to be kept cool and rather below the temperature one would want in the living room to be comfortable. A dry atmosphere is another condition that does not help to keep a cyclamen looking its best. These two important factors of heat and dry air are the reasons why cyclamen leaves are prone to go yellow.

In the winter, when one wants the plants in the warm living room, good light is essential and the December and January sunshine which may fall on them will do no harm. Cyclamen dislike temperatures that fluctuate widely and it is difficult for a plant if living rooms are hot and dry in the evenings and cool down rapidly when one has gone to bed. The best conditions are an even temperature not above 60°F. (15·5°C.), fresh air and a slightly moist atmosphere and the avoidance of draughts as much as possible. This mixture of conditions is normally found in a bedroom or possibly the hall, but when the plant is in the living room give it the best lit situation and place it as far away as possible from any source of heating whether it be fire or radiator.

Watering should be as limited as possible. If the soil gets too wet the leaves will go yellow more quickly than if the plant is on the dry side. When it is too dry the flowers will flag and fall sideways. This is bad but the plant, on being watered, will pick up fairly soon. This is not as bad as a plant that is too wet; this will lead to disaster, with leaves all yellowing and the unopened buds rotting off, and in fact the whole plant might rot. One's only hope in this case is to dry the plant out, which will take time, and when it shows signs of drying out give it only the minimum of water. The soil should never be more than moist, which in practice means watering in small amounts at fairly frequent intervals.

31

Fig. 18. Cyclamen
Silver Leaf Strain

The leaves like being sponged gently or lightly sprayed which helps to keep a moist atmosphere around the plant. Do not let water get on to the flowers. Another point of importance is how the corm is placed in the pot. If it is above the surface of the soil then the water will not run into the centre of the corm. When it is just below the surface of the soil it is best to let it take water up from the base of the pot. This can be done by standing the plant in a saucer with just a little water in it which will be taken up fairly quickly; say in the same day. To stand it in deep water which is always there is wrong; no plant should remain permanently standing in water. There is no need to feed a cyclamen plant when it is in full growth and in its prime.

A good method is to put your plant in a bowl filled with damp moss or peat. This will create a moist atmosphere around the plant and one is able to keep it on the dry side which means less watering.

The modern silver leaf strain has been proved to stand up much better to home conditions than many other strains. It is also a handsome foliage plant with its remarkable leaf markings. The foliage is compact and the flowers rise to a perfect height on sturdy stems.

When flowering is over the plant can be put out in the garden when all fear of frost has gone. Sink the pot down in the soil with the rim of the pot just showing. In very warm dry periods one will need to give it some water but it will need little extra attention. In the late summer new leaves will be seen growing from the corm. The plant should be brought in during early September to avoid any risk of night frost. As the leaves mature and the plant grows increase the watering but be very careful to give it only just enough during this critical period. If in need of potting only pot on into a pot one size larger.

When purchasing a cyclamen look for advanced buds showing colour. A plant with a few flowers out and a number of buds that are low down and not well developed can prove disappointing and may not mature. Buds showing colour are a much safer proposition.

Hydrangeas
One of the best shrubs grown as a flowering pot plant is the hydrangea. This plant is most suitable for use by the decorators and it makes a most attractive plant for the home.

The modern colour range is vast and one can choose a hydrangea from the deep reds to the palest pink. There are white ones and in the blues one has a choice of all the mauves and blues from the deepest purple to sky blue. Another attraction of buying a hydrangea in bloom is in being able to plant it out in the garden when the flowers are finished. Hydrangeas in gardens are wonderful value for colour right through the summer and up to the time when the frosts come.

The "lace cap" kinds have become very popular and are now being grown as pot plants to meet the demand. Plants are usually forced in five-inch pots, and are to be seen in flower from late March and through the early part of the summer. A hydrangea bought in flower should be placed in a very well lit situation. In a dark part of the room it will tend to lose its colour, especially a blue one. The plant will take a lot of water because it dries out quickly. If a plant is healthy and the pot is full of root, one of the best ways to make sure it has all the water it needs is to plunge it in a bucket of water and wait for the air bubbles to cease coming out of the pot. If the weather is very warm and the plant is getting sunshine through a window it may be necessary to do this twice a week. Never stand a plant in deep water for any length of time, this would be far too much and the roots at the base of the pot would be killed.

Hydrangeas do not require great heat at any stage in their life and, as already said, can be planted outside in the garden. If the plant in the pot has base shoots showing good growth, then the branches that have finished flowering can be cut right back. If there are no basal shoots, prune the flowering branches back by about half. Hydrangeas in the open do best in a position which only gets the sunshine for part of the day, a westerly and south westerly aspect is best. Hydrangeas do not mind a heavy soil but to give them a good start add some peat or leafmould and a little sand in the hole when planting out. If the season is dry and there is a drought, make sure that the plant has water. When planting make sure to plant very firmly and tread it in well.

Established hydrangeas are greedy for feed and respond to generous feeding. Like rose bushes, a good mulch of horse manure or a mulch of peat with a balanced fertilizer would be suitable.

Do not prune a plant in the winter but leave the dead heads on as they give protection from frost to the buds below. Bracken can also be used over the plant as further protection against frosts. Prune the main branches in mid April and cut back to a good plump pair of buds. Remove all weak and spindly growth to the base.

As a plant matures, one will notice the first year growths are smooth and of a soft brown colour. Two-year-old growth is rough wooded and grey brown, and third year growth is grey and very gnarled. If there is sufficient growth of first and second year, cut back to the base of the plant all third year growth, which has become too old to produce quality flowers.

The ability to obtain blue hydrangeas will depend on the presence of aluminium in the soil and on the plant being able to take it up through the roots. Where soil has a high content of lime it is difficult, even by adding colourant, to get a good blue. Where blue is wanted, alum crystals should be worked into the roots twice a year. Four ounces of the colourant should be top dressed around the plant at the end of February and again at the beginning of November. It is no use to try to turn a white hydrangea blue as it will not react; only the pink ones will respond. Usually the pale pinks turn to true blue and the more red ones will turn to purple. In reverse, if the soil is very acid, the pink hydrangeas tend to turn a mauve-blue and if a clear pink or red is required, then lime should be applied to preserve a good pink colour.

Poinsettia

Euphorbia pulcherrima is the botanical name of the poinsettia. It was Dr J. R. Poinsett who first discovered the plant in the late 1820's in Mexico. It was shown for the first time in 1829 at the Pennsylvania Horticultural Society.

Poinsettias in the wild grow as large shrubs or small trees and, before the discovery of chemical dwarfing compounds, grew too tall to be grown as pot plants. In Victorian times they were massed in very large rooms or hallways but were mostly used as cut flowers.

Great strides have now been made with the self branching varieties in red, pink and white. The dwarfing compounds keep the plants short and bushy and in consequence the poinsettia has become one of the most popular flowering pot plants for Christmas. The Mikkelsen strains are

34

Fig. 19. Poinsettia
'Mikkelrochford'

excellent for standing up to winter conditions whereas the older varieties were so delicate they lost their leaves very quickly and had a very short life.

The 'Mikkelrochford' poinsettia is well known for its very bright scarlet bracts with good dark green leaves that hold well even in difficult conditions. Its self branching habit makes it a graceful plant and in a 5½-inch (14 cm) pot one can expect five or six heads of equal size.

The first Mikkelsen varieties were introduced into this country in 1964 and it was from 'Paul Mikkelsen' that the red sport now known as 'Mikkelrochford' appeared in 1969. Since then the pink and white have sported from the red. An even brighter red with vigorous root action has now come on the market called 'Mikkelrochford Improved' and in 1973 a new deep pink will be seen and will no doubt take over from the present pink variety.

Poinsettias grow well in a temperature of around 50°F. (10°C.), but the ideal temperature will fluctuate between 60°F. (15·5°C.) and 65°F. (18·5°C.) in the daytime with a drop of 5° at night. If these conditions are provided, then plants will remain in good condition for a very long time. In the United States the poinsettia is as essential a part of the Christmas decorations as holly is to us in this country. Now that these long-lasting varieties have been introduced, it is rapidly finding popularity in Europe. A poinsettia bought in flower will have been well fed and should not be given any further feeding during the time one is enjoying the flowers. When flowering has finished the heads should be cut off and the plant kept almost dry.

In April one can begin to water the plant freely and the root system will soon become active. It may be wise to pot on this year-old poinsettia and a compost of John Innes No. 3 is advisable. Pot on in a pot one size larger. It is a great mistake to overpot any plant. It will probably be necessary to prune the bracts back, in which case cut each bract back to about 2 to 3 inches (5-7cm). If one has a heated greenhouse it is possible to take cuttings from the old plant. The shoots should be allowed to grow to 3 or 4 inches long (7-10cm) and are then cut off from the old stem. Dip the bottom of the cuttings in powdered charcoal to stop the bleeding of the latex, i.e. the white fluid that all euphorbias have in their stems.

Insert the cuttings in a mixture of half peat and half sharp sand. Keep them warm in a constant atmosphere. Once rooted, they should be potted into small 2½-inch (6·35 cm) pots in John Innes No. 1 and, when full of roots, on into larger pots in John Innes No. 3. The minimum temperature for success must be 60°F. (15·5°C.). The dwarfing chemicals are only used by commercial growers, so one's plants will be considerably taller than those purchased in full flower.

Saintpaulia (*The African Violet*)

African violets have all come from the original *Saintpaulia ionantha*, a native of Tanzania. This was a remarkable find of a plant that has a world wide popularity. It can be found from sea level up to an altitude of 3,000 feet.

It comes from a popular family that includes gloxinias, *Achimenes*, *Gesneria* and *Columnea*, and which is known as the Gesneriaceae. Saintpaulias are shade lovers and in the natural state are found on north-facing crevices. One should always bear this in mind because so many can be spoilt in the home with yellowing of leaves through too much strong sunlight.

An ideal position in the home is near a window facing north or north east. Today there are so many varieties and cultivars that one must be careful in one's choice. There are so many frail and difficult varieties that do not deserve commercial cultivation. The most up to date and reliable ones come from two expert firms in hybridization from Germany.

The firms are Englert and Holtkamp, who both devote their activities to producing non-dropping varieties in many colours. Violet-blue has always and will continue to be the most popular colour, but the pinks and reds in many shades are now to be seen. Double and semi-double varieties

Fig. 20. Saintpaulia

are also produced and one can say these have perfection of form. Star-shaped flowers are also available and these are a recent development. The policy at the Rochford nursery is only to grow the varieties that will stand up to the test of lasting well in the home. Like the poinsettia, which in the old days was so delicate and is now so easy to keep, the saintpaulia which was difficult some ten years ago is no longer so, the reason being that very careful selection for vigour and ease of flowering has been the main objective at the Rochford Nurseries.

With the non-dropping varieties the flowers are long lasting because they fade and die on the stem. When over, the dead flowers should be removed with a pair of scissors.

With a double variety one should make sure of removing the dead flowers as there is more risk of rot which will spread amongst the other flowers and could work down to the stems and leaves.

The best saintpaulias to buy are those with good dark foliage and thick flower stems. Dark foliage plants are less liable to rot than the light foliaged ones.

Those with the thick stems are more floriferous and hold their flowers longer. The dark green leaves show up the flowers very effectively.

Saintpaulias do best in plastic pots; in a clay pot the rough edge of the rim causes rot on the leaf stalks. Sometimes you will find the rim of a clay pot has been waxed to avoid this trouble but plastic pots are vastly superior where saintpaulias are concerned.

Many people think that saintpaulias need a lot of water. This is not so. They do like a moist atmosphere and are at their best when surrounded by moist peat. The plant itself is best when kept on the dry side and when it needs watering try always to use water at a temperature of 60°F. (15·5°C.). Take care not to let the water get on to the leaves as this can cause them to spot. The leaves are usually very brittle so lift them gently and water underneath.

As already mentioned, if the plant is surrounded by peat one will find that, if the plant is kept moist, one will seldom have to water the actual plant. When a plant is purchased it will be in a suitable light soil containing quite a lot of peat and as they are not fast growers they can remain in the same soil for at least two years. When it is necessary to pot them on use a very light mixture as this is essential for saintpaulias which have very small fibrous roots. An ideal mixture would be three parts of peat to one part of loam and one part of sharp sand. Good drainage will result from this mixture with no fear of a waterlogged plant and there is no need to crock the pot. If the plant is surrounded by a moist atmosphere this is beneficial because saintpaulias absorb far more moisture through their leaves than through the root system.

The best temperature is 65°–70°F. (18·5°–21°C.) by day and not lower than 55°F. (13°C.) at night. If the room temperature falls in cold weather to 45°F. (7°C.) then the atmosphere is unimportant and it should be allowed to become dry. At this low temperature no water will be taken up by the roots at all and it would be a great mistake to water the plant. Saintpaulias will tolerate low temperatures but they will not thrive in them. Growth will be very slow or even reduced to a standstill and this is the time to remember NOT to water the plant.

There is no need to feed a plant that has just been acquired. The ingredients in the soil should last for at least a year. Over-feeding will cause the plant to rot. When a plant does require feeding then use a soluble rather than a dry feed.

If kept in good condition an African violet in the house can have two or even three flushes of flowers in a year. This is far more flowering than the normal flowering pot plants and is the reason why the saintpaulia enjoys such great popularity.

6. Ailments

All plants whether they are grown for foliage or flowering can suffer from ailments. Bad watering has been dealt with in great detail, but of course it is the cause of most ailments in a plant's life. Insect pests are another cause of plants getting into trouble. On commercial nurseries one is able to use many insecticides which are very effective, but the controls as undertaken in greenhouses are not fit for use in the home. Many cures cannot therefore be recommended for private homes. When plants are raised in a good nursery they are probably clean when sent to the markets and florists' shops, but pests are with us in the air and in the fields and gardens. Some are bound to find their way sooner or later onto one's plants in the house.

One of the worst pests and difficult to control is the red spider. In a moist atmosphere the spider will not thrive and spread as rapidly as it will in a very dry air condition. The sign of an attack of red spider is when the leaves become discoloured, usually yellow in patches. This is because the minute mites are feeding on the leaf tissue. Only the older spiders are red, the younger ones are pale yellow and are barely visible to the naked eye. They usually infest the underside of the leaves. Systemic insecticides provide the most effective control, but these are poisonous and although used with safety in a greenhouse, cannot be suggested for the home.

White oil emulsions are not poisonous, but less effective. They can be applied as a spray and will give reasonable control. If the plant is not too large, it is easier to fill a bucket with the correct mixture and dip the top of the plant. Invert the plant making sure it does not fall out of the pot, because it is not advisable to let the white oil emulsion get into the soil.

Green fly and thrips can be controlled by brands of derris or pyrethrum dust preparations, which are absolutely safe to use.

Mildew is another ailment, and where leaves are badly affected they are best removed and then the plant sprayed with a fungicidal spray. Dinocap is a well-known and proved fungicide and should be used at fortnightly intervals. Hydrangeas and begonias are very prone to mildew and the ideal conditions for this disease to thrive are too much moisture at low temperature.

Scale insects and mealy bug are two more pests to look for. Scale looks like minute brown lumps usually found on the underside of leaves, clustering around the mid rib. These can easily be picked off. Mealy bugs are usually protected in a ball of fluffy white wool while they are hatching. When fully grown they are about an eighth of an inch long. They love to get down in the axil of the leaf where it joins the stem. *Dieffenbachia* and *Aglaonema* offer good hiding places.

A paint brush dipped in white oil emulsion will normally kill mealy bug, and of course, a lot can be removed with a brush or a matchstick.

One should inspect one's plants once a fortnight which means one should never be caught with a bad infestation. Most of these pests are not very widespread among pot plants kept in the home, but they can be a great nuisance in greenhouses. A good nursery with a clean reputation will have its own pest control staff inspecting plants all the time.

Finally, slugs and tiny snails can hide away in the drainage holes of the pots and it is wise to inspect any new plants that are brought into the house for these.

7. Hydroponics

Growing plants in water instead of soil has been attempted since the seventeenth century, but until recently it was used as a laboratory technique, except for growing hyacinths in a bulb jar. In the last thirty or forty years most of the problems such as a build up of toxic chemicals in the solution have been overcome and in the last decade water culture methods have been developed for growing houseplants.

There are several systems now available, and all to some extent simplify the care of the plant. This is welcome progress in particular for plants grown in offices and other public places, but it is also successful for plants in the home.

Plants already growing in a water culture system may be bought from florists or garden centres, but it is also possible to pot up your own plants.

The most common system of water culture available in this country at present is Hydroculture and in this the plant's roots are supported in the container by specially treated granules. These are made from London blue clay heated to a very high temperature, and then cooled. They are about ½ inch diameter (1-1·5cm), and tiny bubbles of air are trapped inside. The outer coating is smooth and light brown and it can absorb about a third of the granule's weight in water.

The relatively small size of the granules used in water culture means that there is a greater surface area over which the water can be drawn for the reservoir below to reach the roots. The water reservoir covers only the bottom three inches of the growing pots, and all the granules are naturally moist but not immersed in water.The principle reason for the success of water-grown plants, is the considerable amount of oxygen available at the roots.

The other essential ingredient for water culture is the fertilizer solution. Various formulations of fertilizers for use with water culture systems are available. For Hydroculture a complete fertilizer is used, that is one that contains all the chemicals needed for healthy growth of the plant, and it is made up in such a way that these nutrients become

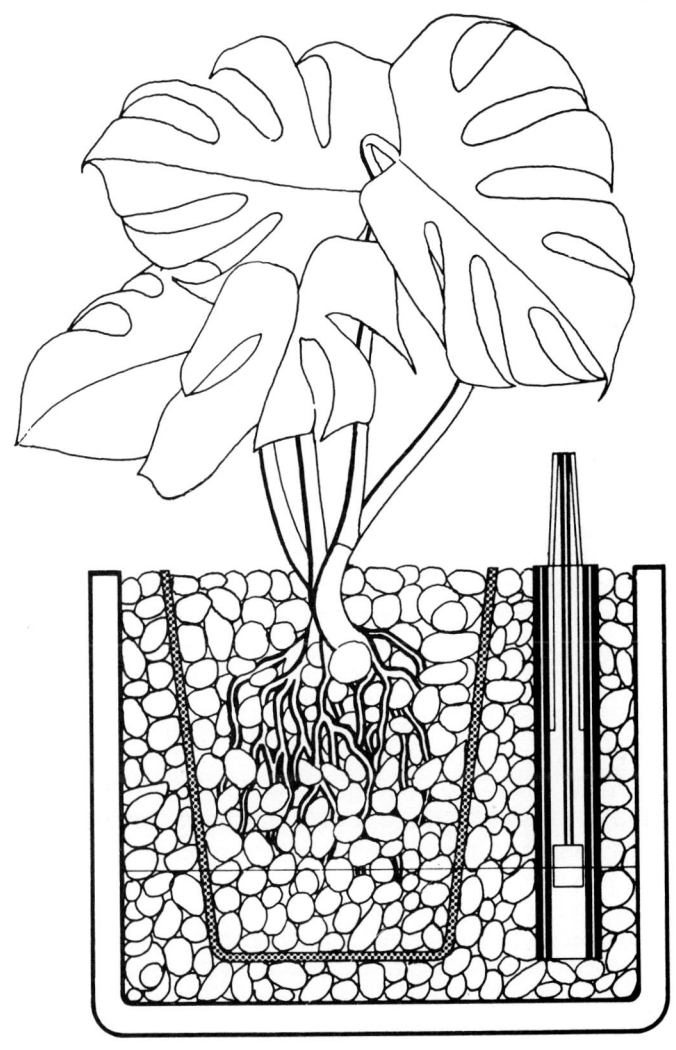

Fig. 21. Above: A sectional line drawing showing the plant's roots surrounded by clay granules. The horizontal line about a third of the way up the pot represents the level of water in the container, and on the right of the plant is an indicator to show when more water is required, combined with a feed input tube.

gradually available in the solution around the plant's roots over several months. As the pH (a measure of acidity/alkalinity of the soil solution) changes so the fertilizer is released and made available.

Other systems of water culture use other substrates in the container for root support, such as sand, peat, plastic (eg Rockwool) or vermiculite. This layer of support occupies two-thirds of the container, and is held in place by a mesh "shelf" above a reservoir of water below. A wick transfers the water from the reservoir to the shelf and so to the substrate around the plants roots. These are not, in a strict sense, water culture systems, but halfway to it, as the roots are growing in a damp "substrate".

For these systems too a special houseplant fertilizer will need to be used, but its application is not as foolproof as with the Hydroculture system. With all fertilizer application, be sure to follow the maker's recommendations.

When establishing plants in Hydroculture in the nursery the usual practice is to take a reasonably mature plant that is well-rooted in soil and to wash off all of the latter from around the roots—any soil that remains can cause toxicity problems at a later date that could be fatal.

The roots are given a final rinse in clear water before they are carefully suspended in the centre of a Hydroculture growing pot (one with additional holes around the base) while the pot is filled with the special pebbles. It is important to ensure that the plant stands in the granules at the same depth as it did in its potful of compost. Leaves, or leaf stalks, that are below the level of the granules will usually die off.

The size of plant being converted will dictate the dimension of the container into which it is introduced, there being no benefit in placing a very small plant in an excessively large pot.

From the time plants are converted until they have become fully established on their water roots, which are much fatter and more succulent than those produced in soil substrate, a period of some six to eight weeks elapses.

During the conversion time plants are placed in beds of aerated running water (about 3 inch depth), the nutrient level of the water is regularly checked and fertilizer added if required.

After some two months plants can be removed from the flowing water and placed in their decorative outer containers with appropriate amount of fertilizer, in which they will be sold.

Some of the outer containers are specially made for the purpose and have built-in indicators that make it possible to see if water is required. This is obviously a tremendous advantage when compared to the hit and miss procedure that prevails in respect of soil-grown plants being tended by the average householder!

Fig. 22. A plant of Dieffenbachia, growing in a small container suitable for a desk or table top.

Besides the custom-built container, one can use almost any receptacle that is watertight and deep enough to accommodate the plant. Small pegulator indicators can be utilised for such containers or one can get containers with sight-glass control. Anyway, whatever is decided upon, there are numerous methods whereby one can check water levels and there will doubtless be many more introduced as time goes on. The

Fig. 23. A mixed collection of plants growing in a Hydroculture.

important requirement, however, regardless of the type of indicator, is to ensure that the container is topped up to the maximum and then left to sink to the minimum before recharging. To allow maximum aeration of the root system the water level should remain on minimum for 5 to 7 days before the container is replenished. When refilling with water it is essential that it should not be too cold (preferably at room temperature), particularly in winter, and that tap water is used. Another precaution when adding water in winter is that the reservoir should not be filled beyond the half-way mark on the water level indicator. The chemicals in tap water will act as a catalytic agent to activate the fertiliser, which is most essential. If use of chemical-free rain water is unavoidable, then one should add a few drops of conventional fertilizer to the rain water to act as a catalyst.

Hydroculture plants require almost exactly the same growing conditions as conventional soil-grown plants, with the important exception that a slightly higher air temperature is required in winter. Higher air temperature will keep the water in the container a little

Fig. 24. Another example of mixed planting in a floor standing container.

warmer—an important requirement.

Besides single plants in an individual container, one may group several plants in a larger receptacle, but it is important to ensure that all the pots placed in such a container are of the same depth. If this is not the case proper control of water to all plants will be impossible.

The grouping of plants in this manner has proved to be especially successful as far as plant growth is concerned—the frequent problem being one of plants becoming overgrown rather than candidates for the dustbin!

Although plants play an important part in relieving the severity of modern, open-plan offices, in their many shapes and colours they are brought to the notice of millions of office workers throughout their working day—people who might not otherwise notice the beauty and pleasure of having plants around.

Plants in water culture generally grow more actively than those in soil culture, and in time the top growth may become out of proportion to the size of container.

I know of plants of *Ficus benjamina* 10 feet high (3m) growing well although their roots are in 9-inch containers (22·5cm). If such plants are regularly fed they will not suffer, but if they become top-heavy or look out of proportion in their container then they can be moved.

This can be done at any time of the year, although early summer is the optimum. Lift the plant from its container and place it in the new container so that it is at the same depth as before. As this new container will be deeper and wider, place a layer of pebbles in the bottom to allow the plant to sit at the same level, and fill in the space between the sides of the container and the plant with more pebbles, but remember to replace the water level indicator. It is important to ensure that there is no more than 3 inches of water (7·5cm) around the base of the plant when the indicator is registering maximum.

An alternative to moving for some plants, such as aroids, is to prune back the plants to a more balanced shape.

Index

Printed in Great Britain by Strange the Printer Ltd.